ZILKER bARK!

dogs of austin

stories from elsewhere

A COLLECTION OF PHOTOS
BY ALEX HOPES OF ZILKERBARK

Library of Congress Cataloging-in-Publication Data is on file.
ISBN 978-0-692-05331-7

Design by Michele Abbaticchio
Copywriting Assistance by Monica Hand and Jocelyn Sitton

First printing, January 2018

To the dog community of Austin, Texas.
You are what makes ZilkerBark possible.

Austin, Texas

@zilkerbark

facebook.com/zilkerbark

zilkerbark.com

introduction

THE STORY OF ZILKERBARK is one that must be told with a backstory. I moved to Austin in 2012 with my dog, Sid and my friend, Chris. We packed what we could into my car and made the 14 hour drive south. Growing up in small town Iowa, Texas seemed like a whole other world.

When we moved, we didn't have jobs or a place to live. I'd never visited before and didn't know anyone who lived in the city. In a lot of ways, I was just looking for a change.

My time in Austin began by finding a home and getting a job as a server at a downtown restaurant. It wasn't long before I got comfortable in my lifestyle, and lost my ambitious drive. Photography was something I had always found fascinating, but I was a novice at best. In December of 2012 I decided to quit my job and buy a camera I couldn't afford.

The idea was simple, I'd have to hustle with my passion if I wanted to survive. After a couple of rough months, I found some steady work pairing freelance social media marketing with photography. It wasn't long before I had nine clients and was making a good living.

The added income and flexible schedule allowed me to spend time traveling domestically. Road trips up and down the Rocky Mountains, taking in all of our nation's beauty. After one long trip, I began to wonder what it would be like to start a business in the most beautiful area of the world.

At the time, my dog Sid had an Instagram with 20k followers. He was the light of my life. My little adventure mutt. He was down for whatever, and I felt confident he'd love life in Croatia. Split, to be exact. We planned to move to Split in June of 2014 for a number of reasons. My research suggested it was beautiful, cheap, english speaking and full of tourism.

On the last day of April 2014, I was moving out of my house. The plan was to live with a friend for a month before officially leaving for Croatia in June. That day I sold everything I owned, with the exception of a few things and my car. At about 1:00am I packed what I had left into my car. It was at the time that I realized Sid wasn't by my side.

I called for him, but he didn't answer. It was not like him to wander, and he always came when I called. I began to worry. The nearest busy street was nearly a half mile away. I thought I would go to the worst case scenario and work my way back. That's when I found Sid. Lying lifeless in the middle of the road. When I got to him, I saw that he had released his bowels and was bleeding from the mouth.

I went into a panic and didn't know what to do. I got Sid to the emergency vet with the help of a stranger. Sid immediately went into the back to be cared for.

There was no telling what was going to happen. At 7:00am the next morning I went to talk with the vet about his condition. They said it didn't look good. He would need two major surgeries to repair his herniated diaphragm. He also had four broken ribs, a punctured lung and his spleen was sliced in half.

I was a wreck and didn't know what to do. Reluctantly, I made a post on his Instagram account telling the story of what had happened. And I'm so glad I did.

Not only did we receive a tremendous amount of love and support, but one of Sid's followers created a fundraising page to help with the vet bills. The community rallied and raised just under $10k in two days!

Things were beginning to look up, and each vet visit seemed promising. Two successful surgeries later and Sid was back to

being a dog! Three weeks after the accident, Sid got to come home with me and the vet gave him the go ahead to resume his regular activities!

It was tremendous news. I truly believe that because Sid had so many people pulling for him, he was destined to survive. I don't know how I could have handled the situation without all of that support and I am still so very grateful to this day.

Once Sid came home, he was far from being his old self. He had lost almost 30% of his body weight and appeared so fragile.

Croatia was put on hold because I didn't feel comfortable putting Sid on an international flight after all he had been through. However, I didn't own anything and we didn't have a place to live.

What we did have was a few things and a car, so we hit the road. A month after getting Sid back home, we left Austin on a five month road trip around the country. We headed west to the coast, then north, then east, before making out way back to Austin in late December.

When we got back to Austin, I published a children's book about Sid and his adventures called "Sidventures". It was a photobook with images from our trip. A week before the book release party, Sid went viral for his infamous pizza video, which helped the book to sell out immediately. At that same time, ZilkerBark was created.

I decided to take my social media and photography background and apply it to my own endeavours.

While going to the park all the time was nothing new, in the spring of 2015 this would change forever. What made this spring different is that I started to bring my camera. It didn't take long before I was trying to photograph every dog I encountered. It was a hobby, which became a passion. Engaging with wonderful creatures and their owners was my new obsession. It didn't take long before an amazing community surfaced. One that had always existed, but had yet to be defined.

ZilkerBark became a showcase for Austin's dog community. The stage for each dog to have their 15 minutes of fame. These dogs are each a celebrity to their owner, and ZilkerBark provided a platform to provide them the attention that deserve.

To date, ZilkerBark has photographed over 10k dogs!! It's seems like a lot, but I hope it's just a small percentage of the dogs I photograph in my lifetime. Since ZilkerBark was founded, a big priority has been on giving back. We've raised over $60k to support the community that has made ZilkerBark possible.

That money was raised by putting on photo events where individuals can get a photo of their pet in exchange for a donation. The events proved to be so successful that in 2017 I decided to take the show on the road. My goal was to take the dog friendly mentality that we have in Austin, and spread it across the nation. We left in June of 2017, and stopped in 16 cities to host these events. It was a great experience and a huge success.

We arrived back in Austin in December of 2017 with this book in mind. Throughout this book you'll see the dogs that make up the Austin dog community, as well as some of the colorful characters we met along the way.

Thank you for taking the time to hear our story! And thank you for being a part of this amazing community.

- **Alex (& Sid)**

contents

01

p5   the many faces of

02

p59   made up dog facts

03

p77   so fetch

04

p105   head tilts for world peace

05

p129   down to party corgis

06

p145   derpy dogs

07

p165   puppy progress photos

08

p207   stories from elsewhere

the many faces of

Some dogs are stoic and regal. Maintaining their intense gaze for what seems like a lifetime. And then there are the other dogs. These dogs are the dogs who can't hold a face for more than a few seconds. The ones who are never who they were a moment ago. This section is a showcase of those creatures. But please note, some of these dogs think they are super serious, so try not to laugh.

DEXTER, 5 yr American Bulldog Mix

DENBY, 2 yr Basset Hound

JAZZ, 2 yr French Mastiff

KINGMAN, 4 mo Black Lab

STARK, 5 mo GSD mix

ATLAS, 6 yr Golden Retriever

BRITYN, 4 mo English Bulldog
Opposite: COWBOY, 5 yr Great Pyrenees/Lab mix

LOO, 2 yr Carolina Dingo Dog
Opposite: OTTO, 2 yr GSP

NALA, 5 mo Black Lab

MAX, 6 mo Goldendoodle

SODA, 9 mo English Bulldog

PENNY, 2 yr Pit Bull mix

WELDON, 6 yr Pug

Opposite: ROSALIE, 2 yr Anatolian Shepherd/Great Pyrenees mix

GIDGET, 10 yr Basset Hound

RANGER, 1.5 yr Golden Retriever

COOPER, 12 yr Catahoula mix
Opposite: RUSTY, 3 yr Chocolate Lab

POPPY, 6 mo Mini Australian Shepherd

KUN-KUN, 12 wk Pug

CAPPUCCINO, 1 yr Cane Corso Italian Mastiff

TOULON, 4 mo Border Collie mix
Opposite: BODHI, 5 mo Black Mouth Cur mix

RIVER, 11 mo Husky

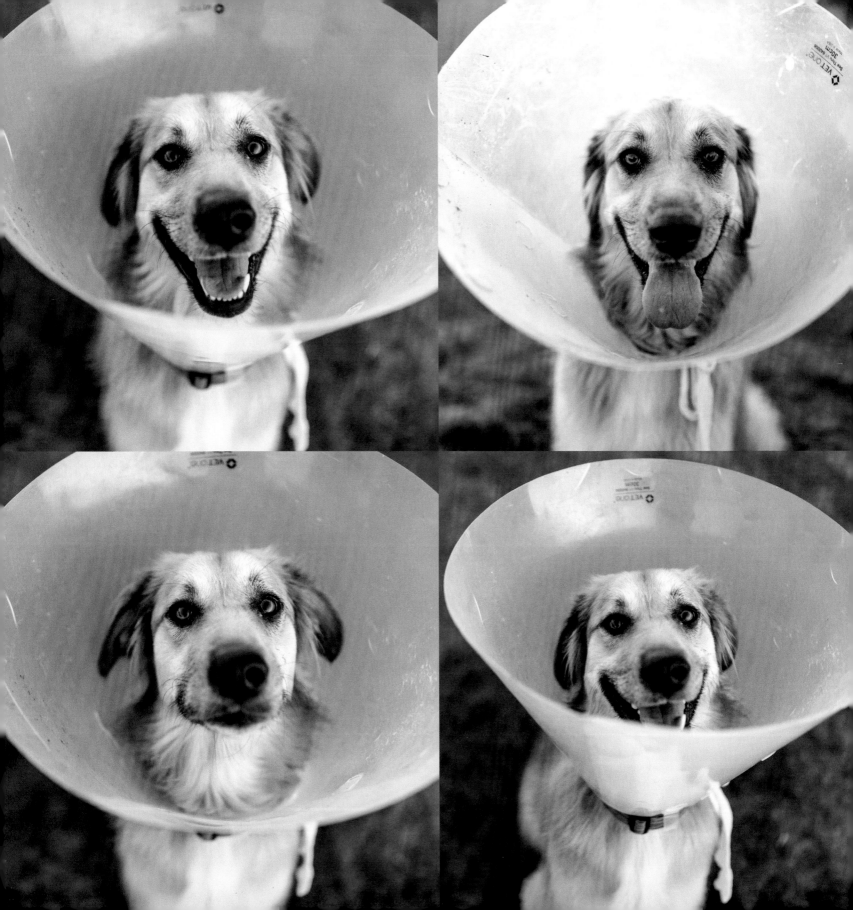

JIYA, 2 yr Anatolian Shepherd/Golden Retriever mix

BEN, 6 yr & HARLEY, 13 yr Golden Retrievers

HALEY, 4 mo Black Lab

Opposite: INDI, 3 mo St. Bernard/Great Pyrenees mix

FRODO, 2 yr Border Collie mix

KINGSLEY, 8 yr Blue Weimaraner
Opposite: PANCAKE, 3 mo Pug

EMMA, 10 yr Golden Retriever

OLIVER, 3 yr Anatolian Shepherd/Maremma Sheepdog mix
Opposite: BENNY, 5 yr Terrier mix

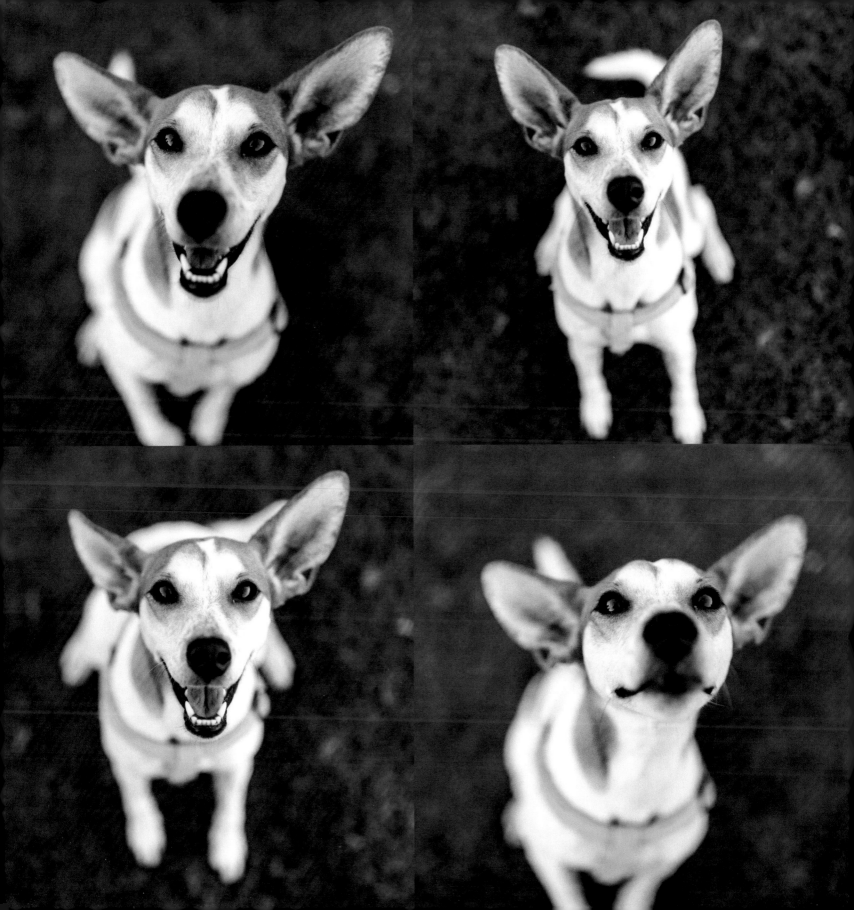

made up dog facts

~~~~~~~~~~~~~~~~~~~~~~~~~~~~~~~~~~~

Before you read on, you must know that these facts are not only made up, but they are made up with extreme accuracy. There is really no way of telling whether or not these facts are true other than obvious likelihood that they are not. However, if you recount them in your daily conversations, it is important that you present them in a factual way. Please admire the next few pages as facts, even though they probably aren't.

#TheMoreYouKnow
#KnowledgeIsPower

MadeUpDogFact #289

Floofs like this are actually just retired clouds
living happily without a care in the world.

MadeUpDogFact #167

Golden Retrievers are puppies until their 8th birthday.

FINN, 1 yr Golden Retriever

MadeUpDogFact #1432

Dogs can hold their breath for a really long time...

WHISTLER, 2 yr Weimaraner

...if you promise not to look while they're doin' it.

MadeUpDogFact #143

Everyone loves corgis because they're
always down to party.

MadeUpDogFact #783

The droopy ears of a Basset Hound act as wings, which allow it to take flight and escape from its responsibilities and problems. This charactertistic is what makes many consider Basset Hounds to be the most fortunate of breeds.

DAISEY, 9 yr Basset Hound/Beagle mix

MadeUpDogFact #54

Shelties get their box-like figure because they
were once bred with SpongeBob SquarePants.

KOBE, 3 mo Sheltie

...Turns out they made for really great loofahs.

MadeUpDogFact #378

The word treat wasn't invented until the year 1408.
Before then, all dog ears drooped.

MAX, 1 yr Border Collie/Heeler mix

MadeUpDogFact #341

A Blue Heeler's tongue will spend greater than 85% of its life outside the mouth because of its rebellious nature.

MadeUpDogFact #12

English Bulldogs were originally bred to be used as cannonballs during the Civil War.

RYDER, 1 yr English Bulldog

MadeUpDogFact #298

Yorkies were originally bred to hunt ants. Some still point at ants, like Yoshi is doing in this photo.

YOSHI, 7 yr Yorkie

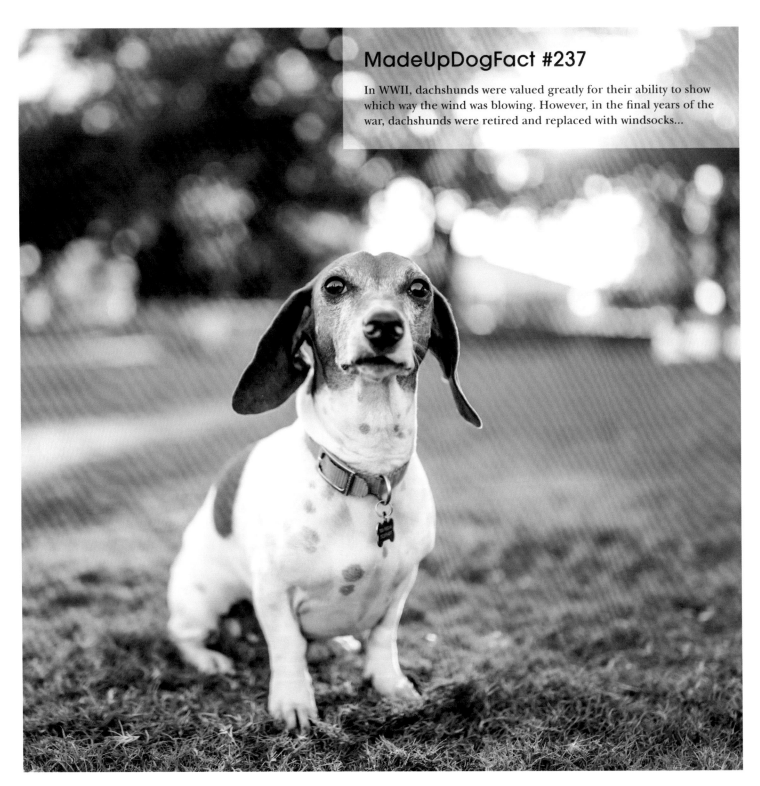

MadeUpDogFact #237

In WWII, dachshunds were valued greatly for their ability to show which way the wind was blowing. However, in the final years of the war, dachshunds were retired and replaced with windsocks...

PRESTON, 6 yr Dachshund

...Apparently there was a shortage of treats and the dachshunds wouldn't work for free.

Dachshund ears, the original windsock.

#themoreyouknow

so
fetch

A stick, a ball, a frisbee or even a rock, it doesn't really matter when you're a dog. This section is packed with dogs who are eager to retrieve.

ECCO, 4 mo Australian Shepherd

mid-air

The moment of uncertainty.

mid-mouth

The feeling of gratification.

MABEL, 4 mo Yellow Lab

BAXTER, 1 yr Black Lab

LOO, 2 yr old Carolina Dingo Dog mix

TITO, 3 mo Mini Goldendoodle

CLEMENTINE, 10 mo Silver Lab

head tilts for world ✌

A long time ago in ancient China, there was a Buddhist Shiba Inu named Doggondhi. In an act of civil disobedience against war and treat restrictions of the time, Doggondhi vowed to head tilt until there was world peace and a release of all treat rations. It is said Doggondhi held his tilt for nearly a full calendar year before succumbing to exhaustion. To this day, dogs everywhere still head tilt to honor Doggondhi and his strides for world peace. These are those dogs.

THEODORE, 7mo Great Dane

NEWMAN, 5 mo Pug

PIERRE, 2 yr French Bulldog
Opposite: MOZIE, 4 mo Great Pyrenees mix

CHEWY, 9 mo Corgi

Opposite: KITTY, 4.5 yr American Mastiff

KODA & PONGO, 3 mo Husky/GSD mix

DAKODA, 8 mo GSD

LUCAS, 7 mo Briard

NOAH, 2 yr Husky mix

LEELOO, 5 yr Pit Bull mix

ROCCO, 1 yr Cavalier King Charles Spaniel
Opposite: FRANK, 1.5 yr GSP/Pit Bull mix

MONTY, 9 yr Australian Shepherd mix

KAI, 4 mo Australian Shepherd

AVA, 1 yr Husky/Chow mix

BURGER, 5 mo Catahoula/GSD mix

RIPLEY, 1.5 yr Border Collie/Australian Shepherd mix

126

WILLA, 3 mo Australian Shepherd
Opposite: TOBY, 5 mo GSP

down to party corgis

All corgis are down to party. It's as simple as that. Ever been to a corgi meetup that didn't turn into a raging up-until-6am dance party? Our point exactly. It's no surprise that corgis have this impact. They're genetically designed for partying. Those big honkin' ears that pivot and rotate in any direction? Party detectors. That dense sausage bod built for tomfoolery? Tomfoolery instigator. The proof is in the pudding! As you flip through this section, please heed our words: It's VERY likely you'll breakout in song and dance. Place valuables and small children in bubble wrap before continuing.

dtp in Austin

These are the corgis that make Austin the Live Doggo Capital of the World.
Because of all of the excessive partying, obviously.

HUGO, 3 mo Corgi

KOMBO, 1 yr Corgi

dtp corgi beach day

We caught up with some down to party corgis at Corgi Beach Day 2017 in Long Beach, CA with the sole purpose of finding out what makes a corgi *down to party*.

Turns out, we received more answers than we bargained for...

A DTP Corgi will beg for your sammie...

"If has more sammie, can do more party."

137

"Plz boop."

They're always ready
for the boop...

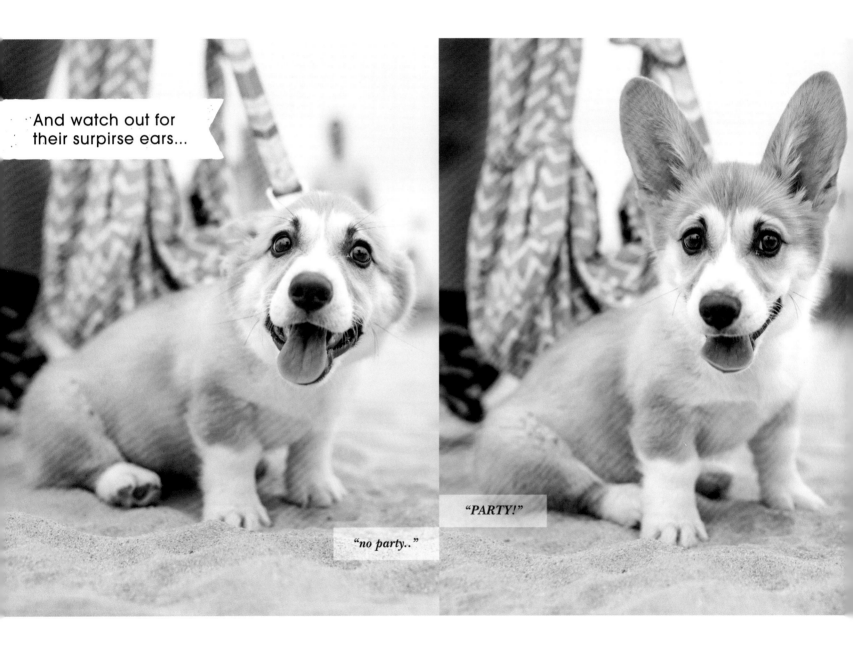

They form their own
pawlitical parties...

"Best party since 1776."

"four more years of
parties plz!"

They terrorize the
beaches with cuteness...

141

"*I will lick your face off.*"

Their smiles quickly turn into party derps...

"I'm having so much fun I'm derping. OMG!"

derpy dogs

This section is for THOSE dogs. The dogs who just can't help themselves. The dogs who are consistently caught making an unflattering face. If these photos were the human equivalent, they'd be deleted immediately. But since they are made by our canine companions, they're put on display for all to see. These are the derpy dogs of Austin!

TROOPER. 5 yr old Husky

DEWEY, 5 yr Greyhound

natural derp

They are who they are.

DENBY, 2 yr Basset Hound

JANGO, 10 mo Alaskan Malamute
Opposite: RUFUS, 2 yr Boxer

FIONA, 7 yr English Bulldog

(left) BLONDIE, 5 yr Golden Retriever/Cocker Spaniel mix, (right) COOPER, 11 yr Dachshund

Opposite: SID, 8 yr Regal Beagle mix & ZEVA, 4 yr Great Pyrenees/Lab mix

eye derp

Blinking is in their genes.

OLIVER, 4 mo Pomsky

(left) NAMI, 2 yr Shiba Inu, (right) LOVERBOY, 12 yr Husky mix
Opposite: RANDALL, 8 mo Australian Kelpie mix

COLT, 4 mo Lab mix
Opposite: OTTO, 2 yr GSP

lip derp

Dogs that catch a snag.

OPAL, 4 yr Basset Hound

puppy progress photos

~~~~~~

They grow up so fast! Seven times faster than a human, to be exact. If you don't take a step back and watch the progress unfold, you might just miss the transition. These dogs will not only grow up in front of your eyes, but they will also later become humans. One of those two statements is true. Which one? We'll never tell…

Enjoy these progress photos. They'll surely give you puppy fever!

tycho

catahoula mix

astro
yellow lab

cooper
border collie

archer
golden retriever

anders
great pyrenees

maisie
golden retriever

stories from elsewhere

We spent six months traversing the diverse landscape of America. And while we never left the country, we encountered an abundance of culture. In each region we found dogs who were living unique lives. Some were eager to show us their talents, others were Russian spies who later threatened our lives. Fortunately, we survived our journey and were able to bring the stories back to Texas so we could share them with all of you.

These are the stories from elsewhere…

This is Bailey. Bailey is a lover of all things.

Bailey

the Lover of All Things

3 year old Chocolate Lab
Houston, TX

"I love all things."

"I really love tennis balls. But my human keeps throwing them into the water. And everyone knows that tennis balls cannot swim."

Bailey really loves tennis balls.

"Plz no. Not Again."

"I will save
you tennis ball!"

"Here you go, friend.
Back to safety."

Another life saved by Bailey, the lover of all things.

This is Oakley, the mini Aussie.

Oakley
the Agoraphobic Aussie

3 year old Mini Australian Shepherd
Denver, CO

Oakley suffers from agoraphobia (the fear of going outside).

"It's true. I do."

"To be honest, it might be less of a fear, and more of a lifestyle."

"I'd much rather do a nap than do a tinkle on a fire hydrant or roll in dirt."

Oakley also has a fear of missing dinner.

"Snacks?!"

Staying inside insures he'll always be next to his bowl when the treat bag crinkles.

Oakley, the agoraphobic(ish) Aussie.

Meet Dan the Iowa Farm Dog.

Dan

the Iowa Farm Dog

2 year old American English Coonhound
Treynor, IA

Dan's got farming in his blood.

"All I know is farm. Farm is life."

Dan wants to show us a day in his life on the farm.

I wanna show you my farm."

FARM TOUR TIME LEGGOOO!!!

"Bork Bork Bork!"

Every morning he spends an hour or two barking up the wrong tree. (Usually this tree)

Dan has been fixing up this ol' truck for a few months now.

Recently realized it has no engine so now just spends every afternoon sitting in/on/near it.

"Turns out, dogs are better at sittin than fixin."

Dan is particularly proud of his field.

"This field is all mine. I've marked every square inch of it with my scent. I drink A LOT of water."

That concludes Dan's farm tour.

"Y'all come back now, ya hear?"

Sputnik the Russian Spy. Aims to infiltrate the puppy community to gather intel on the internal functions of our nation's dog parks.

Sputnik
the Spy

3 month old Corgi
Seattle, WA

"They know nothing of my sinister plan."

Sputnik has been disguised as a Corgi for the past ten years. A Russian experiment turned him into a forever puppy that now uses these powers for evil.

"Sometime I wish to be just a happy pup. Not spy pup. But my country needs me and I must go on to better my family."

"My secret is Bleps, old Russian technique. Bleps destroy all suspicions."

Sputnik's identity has never been questioned.

"Heck they looking over here, be cool man."

"I cannot talk anymore. Go now. Much bleps to do

"Tell anyone of my identity,
I kill you."

This is Tex. He's training to be a service dog.

Tex
the Service Dog

3 month old Golden Retriever
Missoula, MT

Tex is putting himself through some intense training so that he is ready for anything.

"I will save your heckin' life!"

Tex might need to be a lifeguard!

"It's a very difficult job and I have to be prepared."

"Sticks are no match for my powerful jaws."

Tex might need to break sticks.

Tex might need to show people where not to sit.

"Right here. Don't sit here."

"It tastes horrible."

Tex might need to bring you this gross stick.

Tex might need to be alone.

"I can't do this.
Plz come back!"

Tex might need to fight fires.

"What are you?!"

Tex gets his first job next week.
Allergy detection dog.

"Allergy who what now?"

Maya + Munchkin

the Story of True Love

Maya, 98 dog yrs old & Munchkin, 112 dog yrs old
Boxford, MA

Lately, Maya has grown frustrated with Munchkin.

"We've been together for 91yrs. And I love him, I do."

"But lately his farts have gotten out of control."

"I am very embarrassed."

Munckin is very embarrassed.

"No, actually I'm leaving you."

"Ah heck."

"JK you're cool. And I don't really want to get on Tinder."

"Maybe let's just be stinky together."

"Really...?"

Wow. They are really happy now.

"Wow. I'm really happy now."

"Me too. Wow."

Meet Zeva. She's on vacation from Alaska.

Zeva
the Beachgoer

4 year old Great Pyrenees/Lab mix
Outer Banks, NC

"I don't know why humans
think this is relaxing."

To cool down, Zeva drank
a pitcher of margaritas.

"I feel much better."

"But now I am sleepy."

"Beach life is hard. Wake me up when it's winter."

242

Geordie

the Dancer

4 year old Airedale Terrier
Burlington, VT

Meet Geordie, the 4yr old self proclaimed dancing sensation. Wants to show you his best moves.

His go-to move is the classic raise the roof.

"Everyone loves this one because when I stand up humans are like 'wait, but I thought he was a dog'."

He calls this one the wave dance.

"Wow. I'm so good."

This move doesn't have a name yet.

Neither does this one.

Or this one.

"I hope to one day be on Dancing with the Paws."

Willie Nelson

the Retired Texas Ranch Dog

12 year old Golden Retriever
Pacific City, OR

Willie Nelson the retired Texas ranch dog. Decided to make his home in an RV park on the Oregon coast.

"To be honest, it wasn't a tough decision."

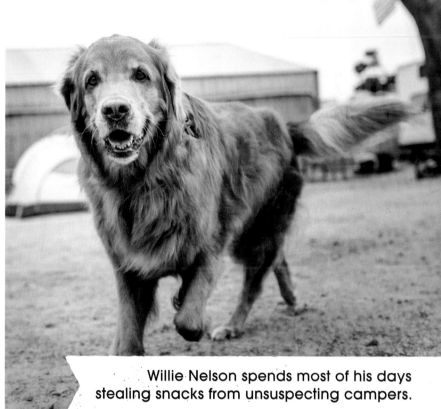

Willie Nelson spends most of his days stealing snacks from unsuspecting campers.

"When you live the Oregonian lifestyle, you get the munchies a lot."

"Alright, alright alright…"

We suspect Willie Nelson the dog and Willie Nelson the human have a lot in common.